For the sake of simplicity, I use him and he throughout the book, so please substitute her and she where you need to. Thank you!

Sherry Briscoe

DON'T STOP DATING

JUST BECAUSE YOU'RE

MARRIED

Reignite Your Relationship

Sherry Briscoe

DON'T STOP DATING

JUST BECAUSE YOU'RE

MARRIED

Reignite Your Relationship

Sherry Briscoe

Sherry Briscoe

Don't Stop Dating Just Because You're Married

No part of this book may be reproduced or transmitted in any form or by any electronic or mechanic al means including information storage and retrieval systems without the permission in writing from the author, except by reviewer who may quote brief passages in a review. This book may not be resold or uploaded for distribution to others.

Chat Noir Press
P.O. Box 663
Eagle, ID 83616

http://ChatNoirPress.wordpress.com

Sherry Briscoe

To my son Travis, and my daughters Audrey and Anessa, who have always encouraged me to find true love, and never stop believing in romance.

Sherry Briscoe

Don't Stop Dating Just Because You're Married

Table of Contents

Sherry Briscoe

CHAPTER 1

STATISTICALLY SPEAKING

Immature love says:

"I love you because I need you."

Mature love says:

"I need you because I love you."

~ Erich Fromm

It's no secret that between 40% and 50% of marriages in the United States end up in divorce. There is always hope in the human heart, however, and divorce statistics are meaningless when two people light the spark of romance and are inspired to journey down their path of happy-ever-after.

The desire for romantic love in marriage is deeply rooted in our psychological makeup. Experts expound on this subject in books, on radio and television, seminars, webinars, and every means of mass communication. And yet with all this wonderful, insightful advice, nearly half the married couples in this country still have not found the secret to keeping love alive after the wedding. As Gary Chapman, author of *The 5 Love Languages*, points out, "People speak different love languages."

So what does that mean? Are we at risk of failure if we can't find the secret decoder ring for each other's communication style? Good communication certainly is one of the major keys to any successful relationship.

♥ ♥

My mother always used to say, "If I could go back in time and know then what I know now…"

We can't go back, but we can make a difference starting today and going forward. Releasing the past and focusing on the present is the first step. It only takes a change in attitude, a change of heart, and a change in you! Yes, I know, you're saying, "But I want a change in my spouse, the other half of this marriage." While we can't change someone else, we can inspire them to change when they see a transformation in us. Many of their actions are simply *reactions* to us.

So how do we avoid being on the losing end of these statistics? How do we stay out of divorce court?

Don't stop dating

just because

you're married.

This is one of the steps that can make a difference in your relationship. I'm not talking about having an account active on match.com or e-harmony, now that you've settled down into a routine of married life. I'm talking about putting effort into keeping the honeymoon attitude and feeling alive while maturing through life together.

A marriage license is not the same as a driver's license. It doesn't expire on your birthday with an option to renew. This is a life-long commitment. It's not a temporary trial period to see if you get along. We do that when we're dating.

Dating is more than just a dinner and a movie. It's when we're open and receptive. Courtship is the time when we learn about each other. That's when we got issued that secret decoder ring, but probably stuffed it away in our pocket and forgot to use it. Dating your spouse is a great way to continue to find out more about him after the wedding. Try to discover something new about your beloved on every date.

It's time to pull out your super-secret decoder ring and use it in a new phase of your relationship.

Pay attention when your spouse talks, especially to his body language. Listen to the tone of his voice. Does he hesitate when he gives you an answer?

- What does your spouse respond to negatively?

- What does he respond to positively?

- What does your partner ask for the most?

How does he show you love and affection? Does he buy or make you gifts? Does he constantly shower you with "I love yous" and words of endearment? Does he touch you every time he walks past; give you big bear hugs and lingering kisses? Does he always want you by his side? What is your spouse's love language? And what is yours?

I once dated a man who refused to use words of endearment. He always called me by my proper name. He said using words like 'babe,' 'honey,' 'darling,' or 'sweetheart' indicated that he had forgotten my name. And he didn't forget my name.

I prefer addressing my partner with pet names like "honey", and telling him that I love him, and how special and wonderful he is to me. I'm a person who likes to hear affectionate words and compliments. So I need to hear those same types of affirmations in return. A simple compliment can go a long way with someone who thrives on words of affection as their love language.

When people express love in their particular way, but don't receive the same form of affection in return, they feel unloved. In response, they show their love and respect less and less, and a downward cycle begins.

♥ ♥

Marriage means "I love you, and I want to share my life with you, for as long as we both shall live."

I'm the worst of the statistics, having been married and divorced more than once. Someone might look at my past and say because of it, my future looks bleak, and that I might as well pack up my belongings and head to the nearest convent. Like most people, I want the "happily ever after." Not wanting to repeat my prior mistakes and not ready to give up hope, I set out to find a better way. I realized in order to achieve that I needed to look within myself first.

I went through an amazing healing process and discovered some areas that I thought might be helpful to others. I know everyone has different issues and different circumstances, but in the end, we all want the same thing – love and respect.

Through the course of my healing work I realized that my biggest problem was that I rushed into relationships too quickly, based on little more than a physical attraction to men with whom I had almost nothing in common. The 'why' and 'how' of what drove me to situations and relationships that weren't right or good for me, are a whole different subject. Suffice it to say, I was fortunate enough to identify my damaging beliefs and turn them around.

If you weren't one of the lucky ones that married your high school sweetheart, and outside of a few disagreements, your marriage is right on track and full of romance, then you might be able to find something here for you.

In this book, I've shared my experiences, as well as results from research I've done through surveys, books, classes, and seminars. I hope that some of the insights I've discovered will be able to help others as well.

Many relationships can only be fixed after some real soul searching and healing the wounds of the spirit. This was the process I found in my personal experience that helped me the most.

With a better understanding of what to expect, and the right tools in your "marriage relationship toolbox," you have a better chance of staying together and overcoming the obstacles in your path.

Marriage is a partnership, a friendship, and a love affair. Physical attraction may be important in the beginning, but it isn't what will sustain you to the end.

Don't ever give up and walk away from love. Whatever drew you two together in the beginning, should be the cornerstone of what sustains you through the years. Build on that, expand it, and grow it into a life-long, loving relationship.

In the chapters ahead you'll find the tools you need to fill your "marriage relationship toolbox."

Don't be a negative statistic. Be in love.

Let us always meet each other with a smile,

for the smile is the beginning of love.

~ Mother Teresa

Sherry Briscoe

All of the exercises in this book should be done by both you and your spouse.

Afterwards share and discuss your answers.

EXERCISE:

1. What are the values that you both share?

2. How do express your love?

3. What types of things do you do for your spouse, not because they are things you like to do, but because you know it's something he likes?

4. For one month, keep a note pad with things your spouse does or says that would indicate his love language. List ways you can show him you love him in his language.

5. What are the hobbies and activities that you both like?

6. What are activities that you like to do independently of your spouse, either alone or with your best friends?

7. What are your main differences?

8. Have you noticed any self-sabotaging thought patterns you have?

Love is when you meet someone who tells you something new about yourself.

~ Andre Breton

CHAPTER 2

THE HONEYMOON

Being deeply loved by someone gives you

strength,

while loving someone deeply gives you

courage.

~ Lao Tzu

The honeymoon is one of the most exciting parts of every marriage, or at least it should be. You're starting a new life with your true love. Life is an adventure, and you're embarking on the grandest of adventures with your best friend.

After the gifts are all put away, the thank-you notes have been delivered, you settle into life as husband and wife, and you bask in the glow of wedded bliss. Do you ever wonder if that feel-good vibe has an expiration date?

While the honeymoon sensation can last anywhere from a week to a couple of years for some, it is possible to stretch it out even longer. Wouldn't you like to be able to have that passion, sexual intimacy, and infatuation remain during your entire marriage? Your relationship may transition from the honeymoon phase to a less romantic and more routine phase, sometimes gradually, and at other times suddenly, depending on the circumstances affecting the bride and groom and their life together. But there are ways to make that transition subtle, easy, and keep the important aspects of it alive and well throughout your entire marriage and life together.

A honeymoon can be short or long, simple or extravagant. It could be a few nights stay in a hotel before entering your home as husband and wife, a week in Hawaii, or on a cruise ship to a variety of ports of call. What makes a honeymoon special is not the length, or the destination. The most important part of a honeymoon is that first step of sharing your life with the one you love, of closing the deal on the affair of a lifetime. This is your chance to give each other your complete, undivided attention before you open the door to the day-to-day life with each other. Take this time to open your heart completely and swim in an ocean of romance.

I always had grand dreams for a honeymoon. Maybe take a train ride on the Orient Express across Europe. I could just see us getting on the train in Paris with stops in Budapest, Bucharest, then Istanbul; or maybe the ride from London to Venice. Sumptuous food, extravagant champagne, amazing destinations, stops filled with romance, all with the love of my life. While that's my idea of the perfect honeymoon; yours might be a camping trip to Glacier National Park, or a week in Disneyland. It really doesn't matter where you go, or what you do, as long as it's something you both love and enjoy.

Of course, dreams and reality don't always match. My first honeymoon consisted of a stay in Reno, Nevada with my new husband's relatives. We stayed with his family instead of getting a hotel room. My next marriage we got married in the judge's chambers in Elko, Nevada and spent a night in a nice hotel room in Lake Tahoe.

Tahoe is a beautiful place, and I can recommend it as a great choice for a honeymoon any time of the year. The scenery is breath-taking, the restaurants are divine, and the night life is exciting.

It may just be me, but I do feel that a honeymoon needs to involve privacy, intimacy, and something memorable for the two of you.

Whether it's two days or two weeks, it should be what YOU want.

If you're planning on a later or second honeymoon, try planning the event together. Make sure it meets both of your expectations, and fits within your timeline and budget. Don't go in debt just to have a memorable honeymoon. You can always save up and take a more lavish trip on a later anniversary. This is what my daughter and her husband did. They couldn't afford much at the time they got married, but after ten years they had saved up frequent flier miles and set a trip fund aside. Grandma stayed with the kids and they went to Italy.

The honeymoon is an important part of any marriage. Make it memorable, whatever and whenever it is.

After the honeymoon, it's common for our focus to shift somewhat. It happens to the best of us. Maybe we start our family right away, or a new job takes extra time and energy.

"Love is not our only emotional need. Psychologists have observed that among our basic needs are the need for security, self-worth, and significance. Love, however, interfaces with all of those. The need for significance is the emotional force behind much of our behavior. Life is driven by the desire for success. We want our lives to count for something. We have our own idea of what it means to be significant, and we work hard to reach our goals. Feeling loved by a wife or husband enhances our sense of significance."[1]

Love is composed of a single soul inhabiting

two bodies.

~ Aristotle

---

[1] The 5 Love Languages pg 141 ©2015

EXERCISE:

1. Where did you go on your honeymoon?

2. Who planned it?

3. What were the best parts of it?

4. If you didn't take a honeymoon right after you were married, did you take one later?

5. Plan a second honeymoon. Both of you write down three possible honeymoon scenarios or destinations. Narrow them down to the best one that you both agree on. Be sure to set a date for it, then strategize how you can accomplish it.

The best thing to hold onto in life is each other.

~ Audrey Hepburn

CHAPTER 3

THE STRESS FACTOR

There is no remedy for love

but to love more.

~ Henry David Thoreau

Stress is the major cause of most illness. It's also one of the major causes of divorce. We stress over our jobs, our finances, the mortgage, the kids, the dog, the neighbor's dog. You name it, we can stress over it.

We stress if we gain weight, lose too much weight, or just get out of shape.

We stress when the bills get high and the credit card debt gets out of control.

We stress at work, or we stress because we're unemployed and looking for work.

We stress at the feeling of not living up to the expectations of others, and most importantly, of not living up to our own expectations.

We can stress because of jealousy, fear, doubts, and low self-esteem.

We stress when our children are sick, unhappy, or under-achieving. We stress over our parents' health and well-being. We stress over immediate family, extended family, and friends. We stress when someone we love is injured or has been in an accident. We stress for them, and we stress for ourselves.

Stress has become a way of life. But it doesn't need to be.

♥ ♥

My first husband was very controlling. I wasn't allowed to have a credit card, or even have use of the checkbook. He controlled where we lived, what we did, and where we went. He controlled what we bought at the grocery store. He controlled me.

There were several times during the marriage when I wanted to do something that he felt would be out of his control, and he would threaten me with the same thing every time: "If you do that, I will divorce you." It became his repetitive response to anything I wanted to do that didn't include him. I wanted to fly home for my little brother's graduation, and was told if I did, I might as well stay because he would divorce me.

Looking back, I should have sat down and talked to him about it. But I accept the fact that I was a poor communicator, and never said a word. Instead, I held it in, and the stress inside of me mounted with each incident.

After four years of marriage, I got a job at a large law firm. One day I was leaving work and noticed the mannequins in the department store windows. The children's figures, with new summer outfits on, reminded me that our children hadn't had new clothes in over a year. When someone in our family needed clothes, I either had to make them or we went to the thrift store.

Don't get me wrong, I didn't have a problem with being crafty or thrifty, but sometimes in life, we want something special.

Even if it's a new outfit for our children. So I went in and bought my son and daughter a new shorts set. It wasn't expensive, and we had almost no debt and plenty of money in the bank. Money wasn't an issue, I thought. Until I got home.

When my husband saw that I had bought new clothes for the kids without consulting him first and getting his permission, he spiraled out of control. He accused me of having an affair. Why else would I do something so irrational? Then he told me I might as well file for divorce!

Note: Don't tell someone who works at a law firm to file for divorce, unless you mean it.

The next day at work, I filed for divorce. When I came home and told him, he was dumb-founded. He said he didn't expect me to actually do it. But I did. My stress level had climaxed and it was the only release in sight. I can say the biggest problem we had was the inability to communicate with each other. I don't know how much a better flow of open communication would have helped in that relationship. But I feel it would have made at least some difference.

It was a hard lesson for me, but one of value. Now I know how to talk to people, to express my feelings, and talk about things before they get out of hand. I'm still a person who doesn't like confrontation, but I've learned a little confrontation is better than letting issues build up to the point that divorce is the only way out.

Open and honest communication is the first step to avoiding stress. So what if something happens that is out of your control? The best thing you can do is talk about it with your partner so that he or she understands what's bothering you.

I'm not a mind reader.

I'm not a psychic.

I can't read your thoughts. And dropping little hints isn't communicating. You need to TALK! Don't text, don't email, don't stick a post-it note on my computer screen. Sit down, face to face, and talk.

Don't keep score. Marriage isn't a tennis game, *love – 15!* Don't complain and nag. All that does is make the other person defensive, grumpy, or more stressed. Avoid putting a negative emotion on the person you love. It's the wrong way to build a lasting relationship. Listen to your spouse without correcting or judging. Sometimes we don't want a solution, we just want someone to listen. Once you get it off your chest, whatever this burden is that is bothering you, either find a way to deal with it or let it go. But don't continually bring it up if there's no hope of fixing it.

There's a fine line between talking about what's bothering you and being a chronic complainer. So be careful. Think about what it is. If something's bothering you, talk it out, then brainstorm together to find a solution. If there is no solution - for instance, if you're just bothered by bad drivers on your way home from work every day - then you need to learn to "not let it get to you." I know, easier said than done. While it may seem difficult to manage, it's not impossible.

Another alternative to working out troubling and negative issues, is to consult with a trusted friend first. Sometimes saying your problems or concerns out loud produces its own resolution and this can reduce the amount of stress within the relationship.

Rather than taking your stress out on those you love, find a positive way to work through the daily tension and relieve it. Here are some suggestions that are helpful in minimizing and getting rid of stress:

- Meditate

- Pray

- Practice Yoga or tai chi

- Exercise (even a short walk or stretch can release endorphins and improve your mood)

- Read

- Listen to music (or play an instrument)

- Walk in peaceful surroundings

- Focus on art forms that take your mind off of things you can't change

- Take a class in pottery or painting

- Learn a new language

- Take dance lessons

- Relax with a friend whom you can confide

- Talk yourself through it

- Eat a healthy diet; lower stress levels and a proper diet are closely related

- Laugh it off; laughter releases endorphins that improve mood and decrease levels of the stress-causing hormones cortisol and adrenaline

- Prop your feet up and have a cup of herbal tea; reduce the amount of caffeine in your diet

- Get a good night's sleep; if you need help in this area, talk to your doctor

- Breathe deeply

- Use hypnosis or self-hypnosis to provide a simple and relaxing way to change habits and relax the mind and body

- Journal - empty the clutter from your mind onto a blank page rather than hold it in or erupt onto your loved ones

- Plant a garden; getting outside and taking in the fresh air certainly contributes to stress relief

- Watch a movie

- Engage in Sex - within a healthy relationship, sex can be a fantastic stress reliever

Find a release that enables you to get your emotional self back in balance.

"We each come to marriage with a different personality and history. We bring emotional baggage into our marriage relationship. We come with different expectations, different opinions about what matters in life. In a healthy marriage, that variety of perspectives must be processed. We need not agree on everything, but we must find

a way to handle our differences so that they do

not become divisive."[2]

---

[2] The 5 Love Languages pg 166 ©2015

EXERCISE:

1. What stresses you?

2. What stresses your spouse?

3. What do you currently do to relieve negative pressures?

4. Don't know what to do? Look for resources in your community or online that can help take the edge off.

5. Write down five things you can do to relieve stress before letting it come between you and your spouse.

6. Consider keeping a stress journal to log when and why stress hits, and what you did to dissolve it.

Sherry Briscoe

Love does not consist in gazing at each other,

but in looking outward together in the same

direction.

~ Antoine de Saint-Exupery

CHAPTER 4

LOVE LOST

Love is when he gives you a piece of your soul,

that you never knew was missing.

~ Torquato Tasso

There are many causes for divorce. One common cause is when two people simply grow apart. What does that even mean? "We grew apart." Were you connected like Siamese twins? How can you 'grow' apart? And then there's the old "fell out of love." Is that like falling out of a tree, or out of the top bunk bed? Exactly how does one "fall out of love?" If you do a somersault and a three-sixty, can you fall back in?

We all have our differences; different tastes in food, music, movies, hobbies. My last partner and I both skied, but I liked to leisurely take the groomed runs and enjoy my time. He was a deep powder, through the trees, speed demon skier. I liked to ride my bike along the greenbelt soaking up the peaceful, glorious day. He liked to ride his dirt bike down the mountain at top speed over rocks and bumps. But that didn't make us grow apart or fall out of love with each other.

There are two very important things to keep in mind in any relationship; what you enjoy doing together, and what you enjoy doing on your own. It's okay to ride your bike on a quiet bike path and let him ride down the rugged mountain. If you're both happy, don't make the mistake of making the other person feel guilty for not doing it your way. Or even worse, don't make yourself feel guilty for not doing it his way. It's important that you do things together that you both enjoy.

It's also important to have your 'alone' time, or time with your close friends who nurture a different side of you. Let the guys play poker and let the girls go shopping. It's called balance. And every relationship needs a good balance. It's also good to keep in mind that your spouse may have, or develop an interest in, something that doesn't appeal to you. You don't have to understand it, or like it, but you do need to support his involvement with it, whatever it is. Of course, for me, I draw the line at things that are illegal, immoral, or unethical!

I dated a man who taught karate and refereed for mixed martial arts cage fighting. I abhor violence and fighting; however, I did attend a few fights simply to show my support, and because I enjoyed watching him. But after the first few tournaments, my inability to stomach the hitting and blood anymore had reached a limit. I would schedule my 'girlfriend' times when he had fights.

The most important thing is that you support each other, work through any differences, and find a happy compromise that works for both of you.

There will almost always be some differences in your interests, and that's okay. Allow it and support it for both of you.

Lack of common interests can be one source of stress in a relationship. There are many other sources to consider, such as the empty-nest syndrome. This can wreak havoc on couples who have focused their whole marriage on the kids and neglected their own relationship. I had a friend who did just that. After 22 years of marriage, when the kids finally left for college, he took his wife out to dinner one night and realized he didn't even know who she was anymore. He didn't know what she liked, or what her dreams and goals were. Sadly, they found they had nothing in common and went their separate ways.

Rejection is an ugly word, and no one wants to experience it, especially from a spouse. We all make wrong choices and have failures in our lives, but we shouldn't stop believing in each other because of it. Everyone deals with their own inner demons. We need each other's support, not criticism, to get through the hard times.

As Dr. Emerson Eggerichs describes in his book, *Love & Respect*, wives send out a plea for love through some very unusual ways, including complaining, criticizing, and crying. At the same time, husbands subconsciously cast their need for respect through speaking harshly or not speaking at all. Communication, according to this, is on a variety of levels, and once again, we need to pull out our secret decoder rings.

Just as we need to find each other's love language, we also need to discover what a wife needs to feel loved, and what a husband needs to feel respected, in ways that are meaningful for each of them.

According to *A Course In Miracles*, every action we take is a plea for love. It is our greatest need.

Exercise:

1. Do you feel like you have grown apart, or are falling out of love?

2. Has the intensity of your feelings waned?

3. Do you do less together than you used to?

4. If you could pinpoint any specific events or attributes that have driven a wedge between you and your spouse, what are they? Can they be fixed?

5. Both of you write down three things in the relationship that bother you on some level. Swap them, talk them out and come to some resolution or compromise. Work on that for at least 30 days. Once that time is up, if there is

anything else left to work on, do the

exercise again. Continue to do this until

you have all issues resolved - large,

medium, and small - and your

relationship is back on track.

You are my sun,

my moon,

and all of my stars.

~ E. E. Cummings

CHAPTER 5

50 FIRST DATES

Love is when the other person's happiness

is more important than your own.

~ H. Jackson Brown, Jr.

Married life can settle in fast between setting up households, working at our jobs, and raising families. In the midst of it all, we lose sight of the romance we experienced when we were dating. So how can we uncover the freshness of dating after the bills are paid, the kids are tucked in and the house is cleaned?

Set aside a date night for you and your spouse at least once a month, and preferably twice a month. Approach it with the same attitude and anticipation that you approached dating before you were married.

In the movie *50 First Dates* with Drew Barrymore and Adam Sandler, Sandler's character is forced to have a first date every day. It's the story about Henry Roth, a man afraid of commitment until he meets the beautiful Lucy. They hit it off and Henry thinks he's finally found the girl of his dreams, until he discovers she has short-term memory loss and she forgets him the very next day. It's inspiring to see how he doesn't give up, but rather continues to fight for love by persistently thinking of ways to make her fall in love with him, every single day.

Shouldn't we all continue to make an effort, every day, to make our partner fall in love with us all over again? What's more exhausting - to keep love alive, or to let it die?

Love, like anything else, needs continual nurturing. If a person means so much to you that you want to marry him and spend the rest of your life with him, build a family together, and grow old together, isn't he worth the investment? Aren't you worth that extra effort to keep the love alive?

Fall in love again.

Realize that you have chosen the best possible life partner, and be grateful to have this person in your life as you grow older.

Imagine for just a moment that your spouse has been in an accident, or by some means has developed short-term memory loss and he can only remember up to the day before he met you. If that happened today, what would you do to make him fall in love with you now?

Find a way to treat your relationship as if it is new every day. At first, this may confuse your spouse, who might ask what you're up to. Suspicious people, aren't we? Have fun with it. Make him fall in love with you today. Let yourself fall in love with your spouse again.

My last husband and I went to the movie together every Friday night. On the surface that looked like a date night. But many times we took the kids with us, or friends, and as soon as the movie was over we went straight back home and he flopped on the couch with remote in hand and started surfing through the channels on the TV.

There was nothing romantic about it.

Having a date night is more than just setting aside a day of the week to do something. There needs to be emotion involved, romance, and intimacy. Make it special. Make it a *date!*

Put some thought into developing special dates with your spouse. It's ideal to have at least two date nights a month. Take turns planning. The husband can plan the first date of the month, and the wife can plan the second.

Don't let yourself fall into this dreaded conversation: "Where do you want to go?"

"I don't care, wherever you want to go is fine with me."

Those can drag on forever. Be strong, make a plan, and stick to it. Do some research; find new and fun adventures.

If you have children at home, hire a sitter, or let the grandparents watch them. Some neighborhoods have even created a sort of babysitting co-op to take turns watching each other's children to save money. If your children are older, have them spend a night with their friends. Make this night just about the two of you.

There are so many things you can do. Have you ever gone disco bowling or played blue light miniature golf? You can go paddle boating in the summer, or take a sleigh ride in the winter, depending on where you live. The list of possibilities is endless, but here are a few suggestions.

- Take a weekend getaway to a resort.

- Get a couples massage.

- A date night doesn't have to cost money to be special. You can rent a favorite movie, pop a bowl of popcorn, turn down the lights, and curl up on the couch together.

- Light the candles on the back deck, turn on the stereo and dance under the moonlight.

- Take a bubble bath together.

- Give a foot massage, go for a walk, and hold hands.

- Be creative; do something you haven't done before, or something you haven't done in a long time. Break away from the usual.

There are rules about things *NOT* to do when on your special date night, although you could establish your own set of rules to be followed.

You cannot talk about the kids, the bills, the mortgage, your job (unless it's something funny and positive). Keep the conversation light and upbeat.

Remember, when you're on a date, *BE* on a date!

Here are some simple steps that can help you reach your goal of a fun and enjoyable special time together.

- Learn to be secure within yourself first. You need to know how to make yourself happy before anyone else can make you happy.

- Get over your ego.

- Be honest and trustworthy.

- Be responsible; there's no need to lay blame on anyone when things go wrong. Things happen; learn to deal with them. Blame is a wedge that will come between you. Skip the blame and heal the wound.

- Be appreciative. Letting the other person know that you appreciate even the smallest of things can go a long way.

- Show thoughtfulness and consideration for the other person's feelings and time, call to let him know if you're going to be late, or do some of his chores when he doesn't feel well. You don't have to make a big issue out of it. Appreciate your spouse, and give him cause to appreciate you.

- Apologize. We all make mistakes. The world never goes exactly as planned, and when it doesn't, talk about it.

- Don't be afraid, don't blame, don't get upset. Life is life.

- Laugh together, watch a funny movie, go to a comedy club, take a dance lesson for the first time, and laugh.

- Allow yourself to be vulnerable and enjoy life.

- Be your spouse's number one fan. Support his goals and dreams, whether they're achievable or not. Believe in him, and let him believe in you.

- Have integrity. Stand behind what you say.

- Be a good listener and observer. You don't always need to wait for him to tell you what he wants or needs. If you're paying attention, you'll know most of the time. And that can mean so much more in the long run when you take the initiative to do something for him, before he asks for it.

- Let your spouse know how special he is to you. Keep sexual intimacy alive, build it, foster it, talk about it.

- Allow yourself to trust one another enough to fulfill each other's needs.

- The relationship plan:
  - Play together
  - Laugh together
  - Accept each other fully
  - Negotiate through the tough times

EXERCISE:

1. Plan two date nights with your spouse. Take turns planning the date nights.

2. Text your spouse a nice message while you're apart, let him know how much you're thinking of him, or hide little love notes where he can find them.

3. Make a list of dates you want to go on, places to visit, or restaurants to try.

4. Each of you write three activity ideas, place them in a bowl and draw one out for date night. *Creativity, spontaneity, and activity equals sexy!* Get intimate.

5. Create a special menu for a candle-lit dinner for two.

6. Recreate your first date.

Don't Stop Dating Just Because You're Married

Love is an irresistible desire to be irresistibly

desired.

~ Robert Frost

CHAPTER 6

COMMUNICATION

By Bill Dovel

Validating your spouse, without losing yourself

"You must love in such a way that the person you love feels free." ~ Thich Nhat Hahn

Communication is the key to a successful relationship. It is easy to say, and yet can be incredibly difficult to do. Relationships can often feel like a contest, when differences of opinion flair up. Feeling understood is the prize. When two people are trying to get the other to get their point of view, discussions escalate. Both parties get increasingly upset that the other person isn't really getting what they are saying. Husband and wife end up in a tug-of-war, refusing to validate each other, until they each start feeling validated.

Feeling understood is one of the most loving emotions a person can experience. The more misunderstood we feel, the more our emotional brain takes over. When the emotional brain takes over, your conscious mind is turned off. The reactive mind kicks in. It is programmed primarily by all the emergency, traumatic, and strongly competitive events in your life. These unconscious programs work great for survival situations and intensely competitive events. But they can ruin what would otherwise be a wonderful marriage.

If we are going to reverse the damage these repeating programs cause, we need to become skilled at having our partner *feel* understood. The other person has to feel it on a gut level. Then we have to not ruin it, for at least 20 seconds, so it can sink in. That is the minimum amount of time the human brain needs to process something. We can ruin it by trying to say our point of view too quickly.

In this exercise, I have listed the steps as positive and loving affirmations. Each one is there to cue us, so these reactions become automatic. Nobody on the planet is able to do this for others 100% of the time. The goal is to increase the amount of empathy and understanding we extend to our loving partners.

The first step is to think of an interaction where you didn't like the outcome. Maybe you didn't like your partner's response or the way you said what you said. Write down, summarizing what he said in one sentence. Make it as exact as you can get it. Next, write down what you said, as exactly as you can get it. Again, just one sentence.

Start making a point of really listening to what you say, and what your spouse says. Do this until you can write it down with a fair degree of accuracy.

Once you can remember the snippet of conversation...use this format.

He said_____

I Said _____

Then practice changing what *you said.*

Never change what he said. Telling the other person that the way he said something is wrong, violates loving thought number 2, as shown on the next page. There is nothing more hypocritical than to break the rules of loving communication in order to get your partner to stop breaking the rules!

Now that you are ready, write out a *better response* by rewriting what you said. Include all the steps below. The one sentence should turn into a paragraph. That is why you only use one sentence for each of you. If you recreated more than that, you would need a team of editors just to keep track.

EXERCISE:

Loving thought #1: "I honor the truth in what you say."

Being able to sincerely get your spouse's point of view in a conversation is critical. It is also very difficult, especially if your feelings are hurt by what was said. It requires that you get the concept of what the other is saying, and repeat it back to him. The better you do this, the more the emotional brain in your spouse will calm down. The less upset he is, the more he feels listened to, and the more he can ease off defending his position.

It is important that you genuinely mean what you say. Nothing ruins this step more than getting some part of his point, and then inserting more data to support your side. It is really important to get the gist of what his point really is, unadulterated.

This step communicates to your beloved that the way he thinks is valid.

Loving thought # 2: "I honor the way you say what you say."

This can be difficult as well. Telling the other person that he should be saying something differently is a major error. Telling another person how he should behave is always a boundary violation. Do your very best to acknowledge exactly what he said...without any added editing. Repeating back the exact word or phrase gets the job done. Changing the words, to what you think they should be, escalates the argument (for example, "I am not sure I like this," being edited to "you know you don't like this.")

This step communicates to your beloved that the thoughts he thinks are valid as well.

Loving thought #3: "I honor the emotions you might be feeling."

We all know that our feelings are valid. That is why many of us disguise thoughts, beliefs, and accusations as feelings. "I feel you are a jerk" is not a feeling! It is name calling, pure and simple. Emotions are feelings. Guessing how a person might be feeling validates his emotions. Telling him how he is feeling - "you are angry," for example - is a boundary violation. You only you know how you are feeling. Write out your response in terms of a guess, or how you would feel. The one exception to this is when your spouse has stated what emotions he is feeling. Then, it is very important to say that emotion back, exactly as he said it.

This step communicates to your beloved that his emotions are valid.

Loving thought #4: "I would like to know how you think and feel."

Here is where you inquire gently. Cross examining your spouse like a trial attorney can be a failure at this step. This is where you are providing a safe place for him to express himself freely.

This step communicates to your beloved that he is important.

Loving thought #5: "I am feeling____"

This is the simplest one to do...in theory. You fill in the blank with a single emotion. If you begin to explain why, you are reentering the argument. Simply state the emotion you are feeling, whatever it actually is. You are not collapsing yourself to please the other person. But you are not arguing your point, under the guise of listening to him.

This step communicates to your beloved that you are sincere, while valuing yourself as well.

Loving thought #6: "I appreciate you as you are."

You find something about your spouse that you really value. Then you tell him. Conflict communicates to both people that they are less valuable than the issue being discussed. Reversing this damage is crucial. Over time, people's love for each other dies the death of a thousand cuts.

This step communicates to your beloved that he is valuable, you recognize it, and you value him.

Don't try to prepare a pat answer ahead of time. As soon as you do this, you are proving that you're not listening. Practice this exercise on an exchange you have already had. As you become more skilled at this, the more it will happen naturally.

The one exception to this is to take a break. During the break, write out how you would have responded. Then write a note saying now that you have thought it through...then insert your thoughtful editing.

Just like learning to dance, learn the moves...practice the moves...then you dance. Free and inspired. Everything else is just a dance lesson. In conversation, your repeated attempts to really listen become a habit. Then your conversations will be more loving and empathetic, naturally.

Love is a bridge between you and everything
~Rumi

CHAPTER 7

SURVEY SAYS...

I recently sent out a survey and asked some of the following questions of men and women. I thought it might be helpful for you to read through some of their answers for ideas and inspiration.

HOW WE MET:

Blind date set up by his ex-spouse

Bowling league

Church

Church-sponsored single's dance

Coffee shop

College debate team between sister colleges

Sherry Briscoe

College tailgate party

College youth group event

Dance lessons

Dentist's office

Friend of the family

Introduced through a mutual friend

Junior high

Lunch with some friends

Military base

Night club while on a date with someone else

On-line

Party

Public school

Through the encouragement from a high school

acquaintance

Work

Yoga

Don't Stop Dating Just Because You're Married

FIRST DATES AND MEMORABLE DATES:

Ballroom dancing lesson and dinner at a chic café

Being in nature, on a pier, by a stream, in the mountains

Boating

Camping trips

Champagne, while soaking in a hot tub under a starry sky

Concerts

Couples massages and special getaways

Doing certain things in the tall grass in the field behind our house

Downtown nightclub

Fancy expensive dinner in an almost deserted hotel in Tivoli, Italy

Handel's Messiah

He booked a hotel room with a whirlpool

He bought a CD with the first song we danced to at our wedding and played it on the way to our anniversary date, celebrated with a bottle of champagne

He fixed dinner for me

High School dance

Hiking

Kayak trip, zip lining, and wine tasting

Milkshake at Shari's

Movies

Oregon coast

Out for drinks

Picnics

Receiving roses and being taken to a small French restaurant for an elegant dinner

Sherry Briscoe

Season tickets to the theater

Snuggling in a car overlooking the city

Soaking in a hot tub under the stars with a
bottle of champagne and the deck lit up with
candles

Theater

Took her to Paris, France

Walking along the beach barefoot after dinner
and wine

Weekend out of town

RECENT ROMANTIC DEEDS:

Back rubs

Dinner on a restaurant's patio next to the river at sunset

Dinner with live music, then strolled along the river hand in hand

Drew her a warm bubble bath, let her enjoy it by herself for a while, then let her enjoy it with me

He's attentive

He says or does things to make me feel beautiful and special every single day

He took me to Europe

He wrote our names on a cliff of sand that he had climbed in Oregon, then put the year by it and a heart around it

I buy her flowers

Sherry Briscoe

I came home from work to a candle-lit dinner for no special reason

I like to surprise him with gifts

I still flirt with him

Left me a love note in my car so I'd see it on my way to work

Sat on his lap and made out – very high-schoolish!

She did my chores I had been procrastinating doing, then cooked my favorite dinner for me

She gave me a jar filled with 'love knots' short statements of things she would do for me

She signs little cards and love notes to me

Surprise trip out of town

We cook together

AREAS THAT NEED MORE WORK:

Be more active outdoors

Be less hard-headed and stubborn

Communication

Continue to find a middle ground when it comes to raising kids

His relationship with my children needs to be better

Keep laughing and find a healthy way to talk about the stuff that bugs us

More open and honest communication about sex

More open with each other instead of being concerned about reactions

More patient and understanding with each other, especially in stressful times

More time together

Sherry Briscoe

She needs to initiate sex more

Slow down and talk more day in and day out

Take more time off to relax

Tell him what I want more often, and have him communicate when he is upset, instead of pretending all is well

Tell the truth, don't hold in anger

WHY A MARRIAGE ENDED:

Abuse

Adultery

Alcoholism / addictions

Bitterness between us

Critical

Emotionally disconnected

He didn't have time for me anymore, he was a work-aholic, and took me for granted

He treated me more like a child rather than his wife

He was demeaning

He was too controlling

He wouldn't grow up and be responsible

Kids from our previous marriage

Money

Quit communicating

Sherry Briscoe

Sex was no longer wanted, or enjoyable

She lost respect for me

She no longer trusted me

Unsupportive

We both quit trying

We had nothing in common

In closing, remember this: love is the greatest gift of all. Don't squander it. Cherish it. Just because you're married doesn't mean you have to stop dating your spouse. There is still excitement and romance in the air, after thirty days of marriage, or thirty years.

It's your choice.

Be creative. Find a way to surprise the one you love, and you just may surprise yourself.

Where there is love there is life.

~ Mahatma Gandhi

Recommended Reading:

Cheat on Your Husband (with your husband) by Andrea Syrtash

52 Uncommon Dates by Randy E Southern

The Five Love Languages by Gary Chapman

The New Rules for Love Sex & Dating by Andy Stanley

No Greater Love by Mother Theresa

Date your Wife by Justin Buzzard

I hope you enjoyed the inspirations, insights and ideas in this book. I welcome your thoughts on my website: www.sherrybriscoe.com

And if you get a chance, please leave a review on amazon.com.